Original title:
Rooms of Memory

Copyright © 2025 Creative Arts Management OÜ
All rights reserved.

Author: Vivienne Beaumont
ISBN HARDBACK: 978-1-80587-012-8
ISBN PAPERBACK: 978-1-80587-482-9

The Drift of Unwritten Lines

In a corner, dust bunnies play,
Chasing thoughts that drift away.
A sock puppet's making a scene,
As the cat eyes the marshmallow queen.

The chair squeaks tales of old debates,
While a forgotten sandwich awaits.
A rubber chicken on the shelf,
Seems to mock my lazy self.

Fragments of Forgotten Joys

Hiding beneath the TV screen,
A game controller's lost its sheen.
Old pizza boxes tell a tale,
Of victories and snacks, without fail.

A jigsaw puzzle, pieces worn,
A cat mayhem, and a sock was torn.
Each laugh echoes in dusty nooks,
As we trip over forgotten books.

Safe Havens of the Soul

The couch, a cradle for lazy bones,
With popcorn scattered like noisy drones.
Remote controls spin tales of woe,
As I search for a show I used to know.

In a corner, a gnome with a grin,
Keeps secrets safe beneath his chin.
While the fridge hums a lullaby's song,
To remind me where the snacks belong.

Gates to a Bygone Era

Memories hang on an old coat rack,
With hats and scarves that fade to black.
Comics stacked up, a colorful mess,
Whispers of laughter in every recess.

The old clock ticks with a goofy grin,
Time's concept lost, a cheerful din.
While dust motes dance in a sunbeam's glow,
At the portal of "What did we know?"

The Library of Solitude

In the corner, a cat yawns wide,
Books stack high, like dreams they bide.
Whispers of stories, shadows play,
I search for a plot, but drift away.

There's a chair that creaks with every sway,
I grab a volume, it leads me astray.
I laugh at a joke from a billionaire,
While my coffee spills without a care.

The lost pages dance, a waltz of dust,
Each spine holds secrets, it's truly a must.
A world where the characters forget their lines,
And I'm the one making up punchy rhymes.

When I finally leave, my hair's a mess,
That cheeky cat gives a judgmental press.
Alone with my thoughts, and that silly grin,
This quiet retreat is where the fun begins.

Windows to Silent Sorrows

Peering through panes where the sun won't shine,
I see the geraniums plotting a line.
Their petals gossip in a breeze so sly,
While I sip my tea, wondering why.

The neighbor's cat plays king of the ledge,
A crown made of leaves, on a playful edge.
I chuckle as he braces for a leap,
Knocking over pots in a plan oh so deep.

Each window's a frame for a sitcom of sorts,
From laundry mishaps to tennis retorts.
The pigeons debate on the best way to soar,
While I take notes, such a lively lore.

I scribble in colors that clash and collide,
Between laugh-out-louds and the times I've cried.
These glimpses of life, a montage so grand,
Through windows of sorrow, humor's we stand.

Secrets Beyond the Threshold

In closets filled with old, lost socks,
Gnarly toys that talk like clocks.
A cereal box with a prize still inside,
And dust bunnies that take us for a ride.

Behind the door, a secret stash,
Of birthday candles and glittery trash.
We giggle as we tiptoe near,
Where whispers of laughter float in the air.

Guardians of the Forgotten

There sits a cat with a velvet paw,
Guarding treasures we never saw.
A half-eaten sandwich from day before,
And a dinosaur hiding behind the door.

Old shoes stacked like a messy tower,
In their shadows lies a forgotten flower.
With every creak and squeak we poke,
It's a comedy show, the memories choke.

The Aroma of Old Books

Dusty volumes with a whiff of sage,
Tales of dragons on a weathered page.
A bookmark carved from a gum wrapper,
Causing laughter from a friendly napper.

Worn spines whisper of adventures past,
When the ink would spill and spells were cast.
Each flipping page a chance to grin,
As we dive into where dreams begin.

Faint Murmurs of Love

In the corner, a love note gone stale,
Written in haste, now a comic tale.
It says "I adore you!" with a heart-shaped doodle,
Next to a ketchup stain from last night's noodle.

Two mugs sit crooked, still half full,
Filled with stories so sweet, they pull.
We chuckle at how it all began,
With slushy hearts and a dance of a man.

Silhouettes of the Unseen

In the corner, a chair sits still,
With a jacket that fits like a thrill.
A ghost of a laugh, a wink from afar,
Just a reminder of who you are.

Underneath the old rug's face,
Lies a sock with a curious grace.
It's paired with a shoe that's lost its mate,
A love story sealed by a twist of fate.

Pictures hang crooked, grinning wide,
They whisper of secrets we cannot hide.
A dance in the kitchen, a splash of wine,
Those blurry nights were simply divine.

So tiptoe around, be cautious yet spry,
For the shadows hold laughter that never will die.
They chuckle and wiggle, a cheeky delight,
In the silhouettes hidden from view at night.

Pathways of Forgotten Smiles

In the hallway, old shoes sit in a row,
They whispered of adventures wherever they'd go.
Each scuff holds a story, a chuckle or two,
Of tripping on air and a slippery shoe.

A mirror reflects a grin that's not mine,
It chuckles and winks with a glimmering shine.
Say cheese to the memories, they're all a bit weird,
Like dancing with shadows when no one appeared.

The fridge hums a tune, an odd little beat,
While leftovers plot their adventurous feat.
With a flick of the light, they sizzle and sprawl,
Who knew yesterday's pizza could still have a ball?

So wander these pathways where laughter's laid bare,
Collecting these smiles, you'll soon find they care.
In corners where mischief has painted the walls,
You'll find the bright echoes of giggles and calls.

Whispers of the Past

In the attic, a trunk with a hat full of air,
Whispers of old tales invite you to stare.
A pair of wild spectacles perched on a bear,
Watch out for the dust bunnies ready to dare.

An old radio crackles with tunes from afar,
It's trying to dance in a rather odd jar.
Forgetfulness reigns, yet it jiggles and sways,
Making melodies sing through the cluttered days.

The clock on the mantel ticks cheekily loud,
As if it has secrets, it's too proud to crowd.
Each tick is a wink, each tock is a grin,
Reminding that laughter is where we begin.

So listen for echoes and giggles that tease,
In corners, in shadows, they drift on the breeze.
In whispers so sneaky, and glee in disguise,
Are the stories that dance in your heart and your eyes.

Storage of Solitude

In the back, a haunted space,
Dust bunnies race with a silly face.
Old shoes talk, gossip spread,
About the trips we never fled.

Mismatched socks giggle in glee,
One hat claims it's the best of three.
A clock ticks backward, its hands all wrong,
Reminding us that time's a song.

Toys once played with, now collect grime,
The teddy bear laughs at endless time.
In this nook, laughter calls,
Echoed tales from forgotten walls.

Surprises hide in every corner,
A vacuum cleaner, a silent mourner.
For in solitude's space, we find delight,
Cherished oddities, tucked out of sight.

Nostalgic Spirals

In the attic, memories swirl,
A hula hoop makes my head twirl.
Old vinyl records sing out loud,
As I dance like no one's around.

The old bicycle's missing its seat,
Now it serves as a novel retreat.
With a paintbrush, I mock the past,
Sketching moments that faded fast.

Trophies dusted, gather tales tall,
A splintered shelf, it's seen it all.
Each trinket spins a funny yarn,
A vintage globe that's lost its charm.

Worn-out linens become bedspread bliss,
Recalling the naps I might have missed.
With laughter echoing in this space,
Nostalgia makes the dull a race.

The Scent of Old Photographs

Faded pictures line the wall,
A musty whiff of time's soft call.
Faces grin through a yellowed haze,
Waving hello in blurred displays.

Here's grandma, with a hairdo grand,
Clutching an ironing board in hand.
Dad's big 'fro, what a sight,
A sight that makes the mirror fright!

Each snap tells tales in sepia tones,
Of pets that disappeared like stones.
A cat in a hat on a woman's lap,
Seems like she planned a grand mishap.

Laughter wafts with the paper's scent,
In every crease, a giggle spent.
Old photographs never fade away,
They just pose silly, day after day.

Shadows of a Distant Echo

In the hallway, whispers dance,
A shadow swings in a silly prance.
The echoes of laughter scatter wide,
Chasing lost socks that seemed to hide.

A door creaks open, boots in tow,
They stomped through mud, but now they glow!
Tickling shadows beneath the bed,
Tickling thoughts that one once said.

From far away, a radio plays,
Songs of yore in a bumbling blaze.
The dog barks back at the radio's tune,
As we dance around like it's mid-June.

Letters forgotten, promising fun,
With secret messages no one's won.
Shadows prance in a quirky ballet,
In this echo, hilarity's here to stay.

Faded Pages of Time

Once I found an old suitcase,
Full of socks and a rubber goose.
It belonged to Uncle Ned,
Who maybe never fed his hedgehog, too loose.

Receipts from 1982,
For magic tricks and pink goo.
Was he a wizard in disguise?
Or just a man who loved fondue?

There's a picture of a cat,
Wearing sunglasses and a hat.
Did it think it was cool?
Or just too proud to sit and chat?

Memories scribbled on napkins,
Like baked beans at family potlucks in.
The laughter still echoes loud,
In this treasure trove of wins and sins.

Hidden Corners of Reflection

Beneath the stairs, a box lay snug,
Full of trinkets and an old bug.
Why does a spoon need a friend?
With a sugar cube, they always snug.

Old hats stacked to the ceiling high,
They've seen more than we'll ever try.
One whispered, "I once wore a crown,"
While I just laughed, unable to comply.

A feather boa, damp from rain,
Beckons tales of a wild train.
"Dare to dance," it seems to shout,
While I just tiptoe, feeling the strain.

In corners where shadows pretend,
Lives a pineapple, a long-lost friend.
Sharing stories through the years,
Making us giggle 'round every bend.

Footprints on the Floor

Trace the paths where we have strayed,
In mismatched shoes and grand charades.
Did that mop just shatter dreams?
Or was it just us, a messy parade?

There's cereal spilled, a rainbow swirl,
Once a breakfast meant to unfurl.
Now it's just a floor mosaic,
That tells of chaos in a twirl.

Wooden planks creak with each step,
Like secrets whispering, "Take a rep."
Who knew that footprints could speak,
Of funny faces that we inept?

Remember that time we did the jig,
And slipped on a banana, oh so big?
The floor was our stage that night,
In giggles, we danced, every fig!

Windows into What Was

Peeking through dust-covered panes,
I spot a pet rock; it entertains.
"Did you ever roll down a hill?"
Or was it just in my brain's lanes?

The curtains flicker with sunlight's tease,
A glimpse of toys from my childhood freeze.
"One-eyed Charlie was once a knight,"
Fighting fierce battles with imaginary cheese.

The neighbors argue about their cat,
While I smile, it's all just chit-chat.
A window into days gone by,
When we thought life was always flat.

Mom's plants growing wild in the light,
Look like they're ready for a silly fight.
"Stop singing, you crazy green thing!"
And the memories stir up sheer delight.

The Echo Chamber of Time

In a corner lies a shoe,
A relic from my clumsy youth.
It squeaks and creaks with every step,
A silly sound, a great mischief.

Old photos laugh from dusty frames,
Caught mid-sneeze and silly games.
Each snapshot tells a jumbled tale,
Of failed dances and epic fails.

A clock that ticks but doesn't chime,
Whispers secrets of lost time.
Each tick a giggle, each tock a sigh,
As I ponder why I wore that tie.

Bottles filled with half-dried ink,
Contain my thoughts gone down the sink.
They scribble nonsense, dreams gone astray,
Oh, to relive that wacky day!

Mementos in the Moonlight

A hat that's too big, twice the size,
Worn by a dog who thought he'd fly.
Under moonbeams, it lights the night,
He dreams of chasing stars—what a sight!

A vase of odd socks sits in a row,
Each one mismatched, a colorful show.
They weave wild stories, let's make them dance,
In the stillness of night, they get their chance.

A rubber chicken lurks in the dark,
Silent guardian with a goofy spark.
His beak has seen more than any friend,
Laughs echo softly, they never end.

Doodles on napkins, frantically drawn,
With ink that smudged at the crack of dawn.
They tell of laughter, a bit absurd,
In the moon's embrace, their tales are heard!

Stories Behind Closed Doors

An old broom leans against the wall,
Claiming it swept away the fall.
With a flick and a whoosh, it tells its lore,
Of dust bunnies waging a playful war.

Mismatched chairs in a tight embrace,
Each with a tale and a silly face.
One wobbles, one squeaks, they whisper and grumble,
About the time that they all took a tumble.

A jacket from a party long past,
Buttons missing, colors amassed.
It remembers the dance moves, both slick and clumsy,
Turning every gathering into something funny.

Behind the door, a cat takes a nap,
Dreaming of fish and an elaborate trap.
His purrs remind me of laughter explored,
Echoes of joy behind every door.

A Palette of Faded Hues

A canvas draped with colors so bright,
Splatters of laughter, nothing feels right.
Each stroke a memory, wacky and wild,
Like a toddler's art, quirky and piled.

Crayons each whisper, secrets untold,
Beneath the bed, where they gather old.
Each one has stories to share with flair,
Of doodles gone rogue, without a care.

A poster of bands, names misspelled,
Wonders how many tunes it nailed.
Clashing colors dance in the sun,
Reminding me of the joy in the fun.

A brush with history, soft and worn,
Slopped with colors, a new day is born.
Each bristle a laughter, each hue a cheer,
In this palette of snippets, joy's always near!

Echoes in the Hallway

Whispers of laughter, a tickling sound,
Footsteps that dance on the dusty ground.
A sock on the lamp, a shoe on the chair,
Ghosts of my siblings are roaming everywhere.

A cereal box perched, just out of reach,
We giggle at how tall we thought we'd teach.
The echoes of dinner, a fork in the stew,
Recalling the times we mixed up the two.

A portrait of mischief hangs crooked and proud,
Where secrets were shared, and laughter was loud.
The echoes are playful, a mischievous spree,
Now I just wonder, who's laughing at me?

Each corner a joker, each room has a grin,
Chasing the shadows tucked deep within.
With every new glance, a chuckle and cheer,
A timewarp of giggles, forever so near.

Shadows on the Walls

Shadows play games that only I see,
Dancing like ducks in a wobbly spree.
I swear that one just winked at my cat,
His fur gives a shiver, 'What's up with that?'

A shadow once served my grandpa a drink,
In a glass full of giggles, don't know how to think.
It's singing old songs in a raspy tone,
I toss it a peanut and call it my own.

The shadows all whisper their wise little tales,
About bubblegum monsters and prancing snails.
Beneath the pallor of the moonlight's play,
I laugh with the figures that come out to stay.

Each shadow a buddy, a trickster so bold,
Mimicking laughter that never grows old.
With each flickering light, their antics ignite,
I join in their frolics till day turns to night.

Portraits of Yesterday

Hanging on the wall, a face with a grin,
A hairdo so wild, where do I begin?
With peanut butter stains on my cheeks and my nose,
This old frame of nostalgia still somehow glows.

There's one with big glasses and socks that don't match,
With each silly glance, it's a memory catch.
We'd play hide and seek, but I dressed as a ghost,
Each picture's a trophy of who matters most.

Granddad caught me dancing, all arms and no grace,
His laughter still lives in that wide-open space.
A world made of giggles, wrapped up tight in a bow,
Their warmth is the reason for smiles still to show.

Shuffling through memories on walls of my mind,
I paint all the colors that time left behind.
With each funny face, I revisit the cheer,
The portraits of yesterday still hold me near.

The Space Between Dreams

In the twilight zone where the silly things play,
My dreams often tumble and dance with the sway.
A bear in a tutu, the moon with a hat,
Each twinkling star is a fluffy chitchat.

There's a trampoline bouncing through candy-floss skies,
Where wishes on whispers become pie-in-the-eyes.
I'm chased by a dragon on a skateboard so fine,
While I'm eating spaghetti and sipping on wine.

The space between dreams is a carnival fair,
With cotton candy clouds and laughter to spare.
A monkey on stilts juggles bananas galore,
While I sneak a quick nap just to dream even more.

So keep your nightlight bright, let the silliness flow,
Each giggle a spark in the night's gentle glow.
In whimsical realms where the funny things meet,
The space between dreams creates laughter, so sweet.

Fragments of What Was

A shoe found under the couch,
A postcard from years ago.
An old joke told by a couch,
Where did that come from? I don't know.

The tattered book with a cat,
Its pages stuck with sticky goo.
I swear I had it on a mat,
But now it's just an odd to-do!

A half-filled cup with cold tea,
Who left this here, was it me?
The memory dances, like a glee,
Like a spider swinging precariously.

The clock ticks back to when we laughed,
With every tick, a silly past.
We wore those hats, oh what a craft,
Now just a selfie, fading fast.

Chasing the Faded Light

Beneath the porch, the shadows play,
A game of hide and seek we knew.
Slip on a shoe, begin the fray,
I tripped, and I fell, right into dew!

The old flashlight flickers bright,
We'd chase the ghosts of summer nights.
The warmth of laughter felt so right,
Now it's a riddle with no insights.

The squeaky swing in the yard,
A memory that charms with its tune.
I thought I was brave, but off I soared,
Like a bird on an old cartoon.

Chasing the tales of yesterday,
Each laugh a treasure, lightly spun.
We wore the nights like a silk bouquet,
Then dawn broke, and we were done.

Ghosts of Laughter

In the attic where old chairs creak,
A stuffed bear one could not ignore.
Its face, a smile, though it won't speak,
A reminder of giggles on the floor.

The games we played with whispers loud,
A knock-knock joke brings fits of glee.
So many memories wrapped in a shroud,
Love never faded, it's still here, see?

That old film playing in my mind,
With goofy wigs and silly fights,
We looped those scenes, quite unrefined,
Now they glide like ghostly lights.

In every corner, laughter's scent,
It tickles the heart, like candy bright.
Those echoes dance, forever bent,
In a playful chase with fading light.

Remnants of Childhood

A crayon box, still filled with cheer,
Colors of dreams and scribbles wide.
I drew the world without a fear,
Just a doodle with a rainbow guide.

The dollhouse sitting in disarray,
Its windows whispering tales of fun.
I played for hours, lost in play,
As if time's race had just begun.

The swing set rusted, still it hums,
Of summer's breeze and endless plays.
It held my weight in leaps and jumps,
Now it sways in nostalgic ways.

Remnants of laughter, scattered near,
Echoes of friends, both near and far.
In shadows and light, our joy unclear,
Yet still we smile, beneath the stars.

Sliding Into Yesteryear

In the attic, dust bunnies race,
Finding treasures of an old shoelace.
Grandpa's glasses, bin full of socks,
Unexpected finds among the clocks.

A coat from a party, sequins aglow,
Dance like a fool to music from 'Shoe',
Pictures hung crooked, with stories to tell,
'Who's the old geezer?', we can't place well!

Cookies burnt black, a smell so divine,
Grandma's secret, she swears it's just fine.
Laughter erupts from those kitchen forays,
As we choke on the past, nostalgic clichés.

Sliding through laughter, with giggles that pop,
Finding the joy, it can't ever stop.
Though the years may zip by, life can be sweet,
In closets of laughter, our hearts skip a beat.

Guardians of the Unsaid

A painted yellow wall, a haphazard chair,
Ghosts of old secrets hang thick in the air.
The cat on the rug, with a look so aloof,
Knows more than it lets on, perhaps in a poof.

Forgotten conversations in the dust on the shelf,
Whispers of dreams, the stuff of oneself.
Remote controls stacked, a programming fight,
Who's winning this round? I'm lost in the light.

Mismatched shoes tell tales of wild clumsiness,
Each trip over memories, a silly finesse.
The candy jar empty, but still a sweet smile,
Fruits of regrets draped over each aisle.

Giggles emerge from the quietest round,
Caught in a moment where joy can be found.
Dancing with shadows, our hearts light and fey,
Guardians of laughter, here to brightly play.

The Stillness of Time

A ticking clock poses, up on the wall,
Stealing the seconds, it finds a good stall.
Old chairs creak softly, with wisdom to share,
While socks come alive in a dance of despair.

Dust motes waltz softly, in beams of the sun,
Each beam is a memory, the past having fun.
Some things get lost in the silence of space,
Is that my lunch? Or just old dinner's base?

A banjo plays tunes of an age long forgot,
Strumming along with an old coffee pot.
The fridge hums a tune, off-key and surreal,
Chasing the echoes of how laughter can feel.

Time sits so still, with a wink and a grin,
What was once lost can now slip back in.
With each cherished giggle, the stillness will sway,
Life's little moments, in bright disarray.

Reflections in Broken Glass

Fragments of laughter in shards scattered wide,
Each piece a reminder of times bona fide.
Across polished surfaces, faces appear,
What happened to the hair? Was it really that sheer?

A toast in the kitchen, then spilled every drop,
The memories swim, oh, please make them stop!
Reflections of chaos, a puzzle in time,
Missing matching pairs—was that all sublime?

In crooked frames stacked, old photos are frown,
Find the one where my pants were down!
The mirror's still laughing, I'm not at my best,
with all those shenanigans put to the test.

Yet through broken laughter, we rise with a cheer,
For life is a giggle, let's make that clear.
In reflections we find joy's sweet embrace,
Crafted from memories, and warm from the chase.

A Room Full of Wishes

In a closet of clothes, I found a sock,
It whispered my dreams, like a ticking clock.
A sandwich from lunch, still wearing a grin,
Managed to charm me, to nibble, to win.

Balloons float around, each holding a tale,
One pops with a laugh, like a fish in a pail.
A rug starts to dance, full of laughter and cheer,
It spins out the stories, I can barely hear.

The cat in the corner, on a stack of old toys,
Recalls all my secrets, oh what a ploy!
While slippers are plotting, they wish they could fly,
To fetch all my dreams from the cupcakes up high.

In this odd little space, where wishes collide,
Each corner's a giggle, an old friend to abide.
So here's to the laughter, the silliness too,
For what are our memories, but fun we once knew!

The Heartbeat of History

In a dusty old drawer, I found my old toy,
A knight in a helmet, pretending with joy.
He clanked and he banged as he charged at the fridge,
Which swayed with a hum, like a reluctant bridge.

The chairs have their stories, of laughter and frowns,
Of gatherings grand, and the ups and the downs.
Each table has secrets, of dishes long served,
With crumbs full of giggles, and laughs well-deserved.

The clock in the hall, it tics and it tocks,
Wearing a face of a wise old fox.
It watches the antics, the chaos, the fun,
As if it's counting, 'til day becomes done.

History's heartbeat is riddled with play,
In corners and shadows, where memories stay.
Amidst all the giggles, the tales old and new,
It's laughter that echoes, when the skies turn blue.

The Architecture of Dreams

A pillow shaped like toast, slept on by a cat,
Invents a new story, of dreams where we chat.
Walls built from wishes, and laughter like glue,
Each brick a moment in colors so true.

The windows are portals, to lands full of glee,
Where unicorns dance, and trees sing to me.
A ladder made of giggles, climbs straight to the moon,
Where dreams party daily, and laughter's in tune.

The ceiling's a canvas, of stars stuck with tape,
Each bright little speck, is a dream we can shape.
As the laughter cascades, like a stream flowing free,
We build our conclusions, in joyous decree.

With each dream a brick, the walls start to sway,
In this funny architecture, we tumble and play.
So let's construct joy, with laughter our beams,
In this comical castle, where whimsy redeems!

Silhouettes of the Unforgotten

In the dim light of dusk, shadows come out to play,
They dance on the walls, in a whimsical way.
A chair with a wink, and a door with a grin,
In this whimsical theater, where stories begin.

Old hats piled high, with their secrets they hide,
They giggle and wiggle, so whimsically tied.
Each table a jester, with tales to regale,
With forks and spoons joining, in a starry-eyed tale.

The couch, a wise sage, with cushions galore,
Recalls the loud laughter of friends long before.
While rugs weave the stories of spills long ago,
In this merry melee, where memories flow.

So let's raise a toast, to the silhouettes near,
Who twirl and they whirl, bringing joy, bringing cheer.
For in corners and shadows, they still haunt the light,
These unforgotten whispers, that dance in the night.

Hallways of Reminiscence

Down the hall where old socks roam,
A pair lost in the depths of chrome.
Chasing dust bunnies in a race,
While the cat just claims her space.

Echoes of laughter, a chair's old creak,
The fridge hums softly, it's gone a week.
Forgotten leftovers, pizza supreme,
Hiding in tupperware, like a bad dream.

Walls adorned with photos so grand,
Of days when I could actually stand.
Now they stifle me in their embrace,
With memories that have no grace.

Plates stacked high like a pyramid heap,
Turning my goldfish into a cheap leap.
Echoes giggle as I slip and slide,
In these hallways where memories collide.

Flickering Flames of Yesterday

A candle's light danced with a sizzle,
Last night's dinner still holds a drizzle.
Ghosts of burnt toast linger nearby,
With a smoke alarm that will surely cry.

Ashes from treats that once had a groove,
S'mores and giggles, oh, how they move!
An old spatula stands as the guard,
Waving farewell, it looks quite scarred.

We gathered 'round, laughter would play,
While marshmallows melted, leading astray.
I thought of that time I lost my shoe,
Now it's a legend, a tale quite askew.

With every flicker, a chuckle unfolds,
The warmth of past mischief in stories retold.
These moments in time, they're never unclear,
As the flames remember, they bring us here.

Secrets Beneath the Floorboards

Underneath boards where secrets lie,
Dust bunnies plot and conspire to fly.
One snagged a crumb from breakfast's feast,
While the mop sits grumbling, just a least.

Old toys whisper tales of yesteryear,
A rubber octopus with a sly leer.
Once liked to swim but now just plays shy,
With a broken leg, how could he fly?

The floor creaks tales of wild sock flights,
Of kids sneaking cookies on starry nights.
A wedged-up memory, bright and alone,
Survives in the dust, a makeshift throne.

An adventure awaits if one dares to peek,
Glimmers of laughter hide in the cheek.
Beneath the boards, the stories unfold,
Where everything dusty is secretly bold.

Windows to Lost Dreams

Peering through glass, I see a play,
Of birds on bicycles, in disarray.
They flap while I sip my morning tea,
Laughing at dreams that never came to be.

Those sunny days when I thought I could fly,
In pajamas, not caring if I passed by.
The trees waved hello, my friends so dear,
While squirrels plotted mischief far near.

Clouds drifted by with their puffy white crowns,
Making castles and clamoring towns.
Yet here I sit, glued to this chair,
With crumbs in my lap and not a care.

So I'll open the window and let in the breeze,
As thoughts fly away like fictional keys.
In these lost dreams, I'll still find my glee,
Through windows where whimsy sets me free.

The Ghosts of Grief

In a closet of laughter, lost socks conspire,
Whispers of mischief from toys that retire.
Grandma's old rug, it creaks like a joke,
While shadows of sadness dodge cherry pie smoke.

The curtains wear dust like a faded old clown,
Each tear on the fabric tells stories in brown.
Old pictures smile down, then they start to giggle,
As memories waltz in a humorous wiggle.

Dust bunnies dance, they're the real party crew,
With each little tumble, they'll dust off their cue.
In corners where heartache once quietly roamed,
A raucous reunion of laughter is foamed.

So bring out the joys that we stash in the nooks,
Let's toast to the goblins we find in the books.
For every lost echo that smells like old cheese,
There's a joke hidden there, oh, such memories tease.

Threadbare Comforts

The couch has a tale that is threadbare and bold,
With springs that sing songs of the stories they've told.
Each cushion a cloud with its own little dream,
Where laughter once rolled like a shiny ice cream.

The lamp by the door wears a quirky old shade,
With a flicker of light that's completely decayed.
It winks at the cat who's plotting some schemes,
As it lounges and ponders on old moonbeam dreams.

The rug feels a bit like a trampled snack bar,
Where crumbs of our joy go as far as they are.
In every old stain, there's a giggle or two,
Of pizza parties and wild hide and seek, too.

So gather the mismatched and threadbare and bright,
Let's toast to the chaos that follows the night.
In the warmth of odd fabrics, embrace the bizarre,
For comfort's a quilt we've stitched from afar.

The Language of Echoes

A tap on the wall is a secretive rhyme,
Each echo tells stories that dance out of time.
The fridge hums a tune like a bass with a beat,
While leftovers giggle in their chilly retreat.

In the hallway, the mirror makes faces it knows,
Reflecting our sillies in flickering shows.
The clock on the shelf ticks like it's tapping feet,
Counting the giggles and quirks we repeat.

A chair in the corner holds whispers of fun,
Where guests play charades 'til the day's almost done.
And laughter erupts from the cracks in the floor,
While the echoes of memory come knocking for more.

So let's unearth echoes and sounds from the past,
In a house full of laughter, let's make memories last.
For every strange giggle that bounces off walls,
Is a tale that timelessly, humorously calls.

Timeless Corners

In the corner of laughter, a chair waits in glee,
With dust bunnies squabbling, oh, what a spree!
Forgotten old toys hold a committee of cheer,
While the clock snickers softly that "fun's here, my dear."

The bookshelf is wobbly, a funhouse of facts,
Where stories get lost in their playful impacts.
A bookmark's a dancer, it jumps from each page,
As the chapters spin wildly, let's burst from the cage.

The window throws sunshine like a burst of white light,
And dust motes are fairies that flutter in flight.
Outdoor laughter spills in, all bright and alive,
As time melts to giggles like ice cream, we thrive.

In corners where whimsy and memory meet,
We'll build up our stories, our circles complete.
For every sweet moment that captures the day,
Is a grin found in corners, come dance and play.

The Hearth of Remembrance

In the corner, dust bunnies play,
Hiding treasures from yesterday.
Grandpa's socks, one green, one red,
He wore them proudly, or so he said.

The old cat naps on a chair,
Dreaming of fish and fresh air.
While we giggle at tales he spun,
Every yarn was the height of fun.

The fire crackles, shadows dance,
A ghost, it seems, is in a trance.
Is that Aunt Mildred trying to bake?
Or just smoke from the last birthday cake?

There's laughter here, no room for dread,
As long as we remember what's said.
With each tale, a grin finds its way,
In this hearth, we forever play.

Lanterns in the Fog

The lanterns flicker, casting light,
Shadows dance in the soft night.
A lost sock floats in the breeze,
Muffled laughs, it's all a tease.

In the fog, we search for clues,
Like where we hid last Friday's shoes.
There's mystery in the silliest things,
Even laughter that Christmas brings.

We stumble on memories and fall,
Chasing ghosts that trip us all.
But with each giggle, we hold tight,
To silly stories that feel just right.

As lanterns sway and fog rolls away,
We find ourselves in playful sway.
In this dance, we all belong,
In the fog, we'll sing our song.

Palettes of the Past

A bright blue shirt, food stains galore,
Oh, the parties held on the floor!
Each color splashed on canvas clear,
Memories of laughter, full of cheer.

With crayons drawn on every wall,
Was that cousin Jake, or a ghostly call?
The art we made, a wild spree,
Multi-hued mayhem, just let it be!

We reminisce, our colors blend,
The reds of laughter, the blues of friend.
Each stroke's a giggle, each shade a twist,
How'd we survive the paint we missed?

So let's jot down all those hues,
In our hearts, we shall not lose.
With palettes rich from days gone by,
We paint our lives, oh me, oh my!

The Essence of Yesterday

The smell of cookies fills the air,
Were they burnt or made with care?
Grandma's secrets, a sprinkle and dash,
The giggles echo, a delightful clash.

We dance around with lopsided glee,
Forgetting chores, just let it be!
Each moment painted with silly grace,
A true masterpiece in a warm embrace.

Forget the dust, it's the fun that counts,
Like stories told with huge amounts.
We laugh till we're tired and can't stand tall,
In the essence of yesterday, we're having a ball.

So come and join the joyful spree,
Where every giggle sets us free.
Locked forever in our hearts' way,
The essence of yesterday is here to stay.

Beneath the Stains of Time

In the corner lies a sock, old and gray,
Once a pair, now it's gone astray.
The fridge hums with secrets untold,
Leftovers from moons of yore feel bold.

Dust bunnies dance when the cat's not near,
They throw raves when we disappear.
Here's a note from an eggplant's dream,
It claims it once starred in a cooking theme.

Pictures hang with eyes that squint,
Forgetting names but looking quite mint.
They gossip of days when colors were bright,
Now they're just shades in the dim twilight.

An echo of laughter hangs in the hall,
Were we heroes or just fools after all?
Beneath every stain, a story's confined,
Wipe it clean, and the laughter reminds.

Ghostly Footsteps

With a creak and a groan, they shuffle about,
Invisible slippers with no size in doubt.
I chase them in circles, outsmarting the glare,
Yet they giggle and vanish, to none but the air.

Phantom dust bunnies peek from the chair,
As I plop down clumsily, unaware of their lair.
They plot little pranks, a mischievous crew,
Tickle your toes as you walk right through.

The hallway's a stage for a ghostly parade,
With chairs on their backs, they dance unafraid.
When I'm not looking, they steal all my snacks,
Summoning crumbs as they stage their attacks.

At night, they compose a small ghostly choir,
With whispers of laughter that dance through the fire.
In shadows, they prance with a flair and a twist,
Who knew the afterlife'd be such a twist?

Shelves of Unsung Tales

On shelves lined with dust and a smattered frame,
Lies a book with a plot that's lost its name.
It speaks of adventures in spaces unknown,
Yet complains nightly of feeling alone.

A cup with a chip tells of coffee's grand fights,
Of pastries that dared reach outrageous heights.
"Once, I swirled with a donut of glory!
Now I'm stuck here, just a sad old story."

There's a photo of me with hair like a beast,
It chuckles each time at my fashion least.
"Reinvented?" it snorts, "I think not, my friend,
You look like a raccoon with a flair to offend!"

The stacks of old trinkets hold secrets unheard,
A comb with a tale, from a bird that once soared.
In laughter and chaos, they sit and they grin,
Waiting for moments to bring humor in.

Unraveled Threads of the Heart

My sweater, once snug, now a cardigan's fate,
Sporting holes like a woven crate.
Each thread tells a story of laughter and tears,
Like that time I tripped over tied shoelace fears.

A scarf whispers songs of a wintery chill,
While blocking the wind during every spill.
"When did we dance with that porcupine?
Oh, the prickles were plenty, but hey, we looked fine!"

Each button with secrets of dinners gone wrong,
Reminds me of dishes that had no song.
"The spaghetti wore salsa!" the spoon starts to cackle,
As I wave it goodbye, watch it roll off the tackle.

And thus with each stitch, my heart starts to glow,
Wrapped in the warmth of moments aglow.
These gathered threads, like laughter, do part,
In whimsical stitches, we weave the heart.

Corridors of Nostalgia

In hallways lined with rubber ducks,
Where time forgot to check for luck.
A squeaky toy still haunts the night,
And tickles clear with laughter's light.

A box of socks, mismatched and wild,
Recalls the antics of a child.
We danced with ghosts of silly hats,
And juggled dreams with laughing cats.

Each wall a tale, a chuckle's refrain,
Of failed attempts and mishaps' gain.
Beneath the light's bright, flickering glow,
We share the stories few may know.

With echoes soft and grins so wide,
In these funny halls, we confide.
Memories leap like silly sprites,
In corridors of laughter's heights.

The Attic's Silent Song

Up in the attic, dust bunnies reign,
A symphony of squeaks like a train.
Grandma's hats dance round and round,
While secret giggles swirl the sound.

A trunk of treasures, odd and strange,
Holds a sock puppet with a name change.
Twirled up in yarn, a cat in sight,
Who pretends to ricochet with delight.

Old magazines with hairstyles bold,
Fashion trends that never took hold.
We handle relics of laughter past,
And find the joys that forever last.

In that dusty place where time sways,
We remember our younger days.
With attic dances and silly pranks,
Singing songs with awkward flanks.

Veils of Time's Embrace

Behind the veil, a wobbly chair,
Where time stood still, without a care.
Whispers float from a crooked frame,
As dust bunnies join the game.

A calendar stuck, it's always June,
With dancing figs to a polka tune.
Though past the age of care and style,
We laugh and twirl, mile by mile.

Old photos hang, faces frown,
A family portrait upside down.
With every frame, a funny tale,
Of mishaps shared in a joyful gale.

In veils of time, we spin and twirl,
Each laugh echoes, a timeless whirl.
From childhood joys to grandpa's games,
But none can quite recall their names.

Tapestries of Old Laughter

Woven threads of giggles bright,
In fabrics worn and colors light.
A quilt of wisdom, stitched with care,
And stories shared from here to there.

Each patch a moment, a silly jest,
From flying pies to a pie-eating contest.
We tucked in secrets, giggles, and fun,
And counted memories, one by one.

With every fold, a chuckle's spark,
For Grandma's stories always hit the mark.
Tales of pranks and foiled escapades,
In laughter's hand, our joy cascades.

In tapestries that bind the past,
We find the joy that's meant to last.
So gather round and hold on tight,
For laughter weaves the colors bright.

A Lighthouse for the Past

A lighthouse blinked at me last night,
With socks that matched not quite right.
It flashed a grin, I waved back wide,
But tripped on memories, oh, what a ride!

A sandwich sailed from ages gone by,
Its crust was hard, oh me, oh my!
I laughed so hard, I nearly fell,
In that light, I knew it well.

A seagull squawked, 'What fun is this?'
I threw it crumbs; it gave a hiss.
The past was laughing, bright and bold,
In the lighthouse, stories unfold.

The waves sighed tales from near and far,
Reminders of my old guitar.
It played a tune, a jolly dance,
In this light, I found my chance.

The Garden of Forgotten Whispers

In a garden where lost socks sprout,
I heard the whispers, no doubt.
A banana peel claimed it was wise,
While giggling tulips hid their cries.

A gnome in the corner, quite a sight,
Tried to juggle with all his might.
He dropped a carrot, just for laughs,
And blamed it on the clever drafts.

The daisies chuckled, their heads held high,
As ants marched by in a silly tie.
"Oh, join our club," they said with glee,
"In this garden, chaos is key!"

A bumblebee buzzed a funny song,
Said, "Life's a dance, can't be wrong!"
With laughter sown in every seed,
This garden is where joy takes lead.

Birthing Echoes

In a room where echoes laugh and play,
I found my toothbrush from yesterday.
It told a tale of brushing fights,
With all the ghosts of toothpaste nights.

A shoe came bouncing with a tune,
Claiming it could dance 'round the moon.
I joined the socks in a heated race,
Fell down laughing, but found my place.

Echoes whispered secrets, sweet and sly,
Bubbles of laughter floated high.
They popped like popcorn in the air,
Leaving traces of joy everywhere.

A tickle of dust sparked a joke,
That made the curtains flap and poke.
In this space where echoes bloom,
I danced with joy, and banished gloom.

Threads of a Faded Tapestry

In a tapestry where colors blend,
Is a cat that insists it's a friend.
It naps on the stitches, a regal pose,
Dreaming of yarn, or perhaps of toes.

The threads were chatting, oh what a fuss,
"Who unraveled this? It's all a plus!"
They told of days in every hue,
Where laughter mixed with the morning dew.

A button rolled in, quite bold and brash,
Claimed it was part of that wild bash.
"Oh, it's just thread," said a silken strand,
"Join us now; it's quite a band!"

A fringe unraveled, giggling loud,
"Who wears this mess? I'm feeling proud!"
In this fabric, a story spun,
Each thread a laugh, each laugh a pun.

Threads of Yesterday's Weave

In the attic, dust bunnies leap,
Old toys chatter, secrets they keep.
Socks without partners dance in the light,
While grandpa's chair snores, what a sight!

Photographs grin, a circus parade,
I swear there's a ghost playing charades.
Mismatched shoes in a corner contrive,
To stage a fashion show, oh, how they thrive!

A teddy bear ponders, where's his friend?
Did he tumble off, or just pretend?
Each corner whispers with laughter and cheer,
Remembering moments that draw us near.

In these spaces, where giggles entwine,
The heart finds its warmth, a soft, silly shrine.
As time trips backward on playful toes,
We twirl through the yarn that nostalgia sews.

Names Carved in Silence

On the desk, a pencil takes a snooze,
While paper ghosts plot mischief and ruse.
A shifty eraser jumps into the fray,
Righting wrongs from yesterday.

On the wall, a calendar fakes its age,
Stuck on last Monday, it's such a sage.
Whispers of laughter echo the past,
In the quiet rooms, such spells are cast.

Old friends in frames offer silly grins,
Each snapshot a riot, where no one wins.
They share secrets in a soft, hushed tone,
All while I sit here laughing alone.

Names etched in dust, oh what a show,
Each one a jester, they know how to flow.
In silence, they dance, those memories bold,
Each chuckle a treasure, a story retold.

Lanterns in the Dusk

As daylight dips, the lanterns awake,
Casting shadows that twist and shake.
A cat in a hat joins the fun,
With a dance for the evening, just begun!

Cobbled paths under twinkling lights,
Ghosts of cooks debating late-night bites.
Pies from the oven, they vanish with glee,
As I'm left wondering, where could they be?

Laughter spills from the kitchen door,
While pans beat rhythms like never before.
A spoon's got swagger, a fork's on the rise,
In this kitchen ballet, who'd be surprised?

In the dusk, where light flickers on walls,
Echoes of jokes bounce through the halls.
Lanterns may fade, but the giggles remain,
A chorus of memories, a sweet, silly refrain.

The Nest of Warmth

In the living room, cushions conspire,
To form a nest, where dreams never tire.
A cat with a swagger claims the best seat,
While popcorn trails lead to a retreat.

Glasses clink, a toast to the past,
To antics and shenanigans that forever last.
The couch tells stories, oh what a tease,
Of late-night giggles and tropical breeze.

Under the blanket, while shadows tease,
Socks giggle softly, life's little ease.
Each corner hums with a hint of delight,
As laughter and warmth blend into the night.

In this cozy domain, we spin and weave,
A tapestry of joy that we shall not leave.
Nestled together, our hearts take flight,
In the warmth of this space, everything feels right.

Soft Footfalls on Aged Floors

Dust bunnies dance in a sleepy hall,
As I trip on stories and memories small.
The creaky boards sing with my old pals,
Collecting our laughter, those quirky kittles.

A sock lies here from a night of delight,
Shenanigans echo in the pale moonlight.
Coffee stains trace where we used to share,
Gossip and secrets, floating in the air.

The cat gives a yawn, unimpressed and grand,
While I chase shadows, oh how time can stand!
Each footfall's a giggle, a tease from the past,
Revealing our folly, and fun that won't last.

In this corner of chaos where moments might bloom,
The echoes of laughter still linger in gloom.
With each silly stumble, a memory's made,
Soft footfalls stumble, but never will fade.

The Weight of Unsaid Goodbyes

A suitcase sits, packed with half-hearted fare,
Unwanted socks and a grizzly bear stare.
The doors slowly creak as I shuffle and sigh,
Each inch feels heavy, like a well-worn tie.

Pictures pasted crooked on walls kissed by time,
Smiles stretch wide as if caught in a crime.
I wave to the fridge, a cold-hearted mate,
Whispering secrets we share about fate.

Leftovers linger, with moldy regrets,
While crumbs from the couch hold our shared internet bets.
The clock ticks steadily, like a nagging friend,
Counting the moments that refuse to end.

Yet, laughter escapes in the faces we knew,
And bittersweet chuckles of things we can't undo.
For every goodbye, our hearts jump and dive,
A hilarious mess, where we somehow survive.

Rewind of Lost Days

A spin of the dial, the record does crack,
Rewinding our days that we can't take back.
I stumble through time in mismatched socks,
Cleverly hiding my paradox clocks.

Pancakes for dinner, oh what a grand scheme,
With syrupy giggles, a folly of dream.
Our plans were a riot, an absolute farce,
Like flying a rocket without proper charts.

A calendar taped to the side of my door,
Each date a joke, and some are a chore.
But as I rewind with a pinch of flair,
The days come alive, floating here in the air.

So I spin and I dance to the sound of our japes,
Crafting the collage of colorful shapes.
A laughter-filled tapestry made from our plays,
In the rewinding dance of our lost sunny days.

The Veil of Longing

Behind this curtain, a whispering breeze,
Frames golden moments that flaunt and please.
A tickle of longing that giggles and scoffs,
As I play peekaboo with the dust motes in troughs.

Nibbled cookies left on the window's edge,
Reshape the past like a wobbly pledge.
Old mittens tucked in a curious box,
Of whispered intentions and murmured frocks.

The chair creaks softly, still holds its grin,
As if it remembers the cheeky chagrin.
We played hide-and-seek while meals brewed forget,
Throwing spices and meanings, a playful duet.

Yet through veils we peek at the mirth of today,
In the nostalgia's flutter, our hearts dance and sway.
With laughter, we stitch up the moments that cling,
Altering longings to hilarity's ring.

Cracks in the Memories

I found a sock atop my head,
When did I lose it? Who knows, instead?
A shoe in the fridge, oh what a sight,
Did I pack it there during a late-night bite?

In the tapestry of yesteryears,
My pet goldfish learned to play with peers.
A dance with the vacuum? Quite a feat!
I'm still recovering from that strange beat.

Pancakes on Tuesday? What a delight!
But why did I burn them? Was I in flight?
That time I mistook salt for sweet grace,
Oh, these little quirks, they make me embrace!

Each memory a laugh, a chuckle at night,
As I sift through the chaos, a comical sight.
With every odd story, I lose track of time,
Cracks in the past? They turn into rhyme.

Overgrown Pathways of Thought

My mind has a garden, wild and spry,
With weeds of old dreams that touch the sky.
Where did that cookie recipe go?
I guess it vanished in the garden's flow!

A path through laughter, a detour of joys,
Where I lost my marbles, those silly old toys.
But in this maze of mismatched fun,
I find little treasures, oh, never done!

There's toothpaste on ceiling and socks by the door,
Each corner I turn, more giggles to score.
Logical blocks in tangled vines grow,
Yet every odd twist brings a 'Wow! Did you know?'

So here's to my thoughts, a tangled affair,
Exploring the overgrowth, without a care.
Who knew that laughter could sprout from the soil,
On this chaotic terrain, I joyfully toil!

Echoes of Laughter

Tickling toes in a bubble-filled sea,
Did I just knock over Aunt Edie's tee?
Echoes of giggles bounce off the walls,
As I trip on a toy, in our grand halls.

The cat holds court on the top of the chair,
And watches my dance like a comedic dare.
I slip on my dreams, the air full of cheer,
What's that sound? Oh, it's laughter I hear!

Silly memories captured in bright frames,
Unruly hairdos, and tumbling games.
Who needs perfection when giggles can bloom,
In the messy, chaotic, everyday room?

So let's raise a toast to the echoes we find,
In twilight zones of our wild, wandering mind.
Crafting the past with a mischievous twist,
These laughs we remember, no chance to resist!

The Weight of Nostalgia

Old pizza boxes, a treasure indeed,
Moldy reminders of culinary greed.
Each slice a story, each crust a prank,
I smile at the memories piled in the flank.

An odd sock brother's in the box of toys,
Forgotten adventures, those wild little boys.
Forgotten, perhaps, yet heavy with cheer,
I chuckle amidst echoes, loud and clear.

Painted rocks hide secrets of yore,
Where I jumped into puddles and fell to the floor.
Why was the broom a knight in our quest?
A chase turned siege in the family's jest.

Heavy the weight of these days gone by,
But laughter breaks loose, like a kite in the sky.
With every sweet memory, a humorous twist,
In the archives of time, a chuckle persists.

Memories in the Attic

Dust bunnies dance in the light,
Forgotten shoes take their flight.
A hat with holes, a sock with flair,
Where did I put my goldfish pair?

Old photos smile with cheeky grins,
Gramps at a party, dancing with twins.
The record spins, a laugh from the past,
A rubber chicken? Why did I ask?

Maps of places I've never been,
An empty jar that once held beans.
An old game console, it's seen better days,
With pixelated joys and glitchy displays.

In this cluttered space, giggles abound,
Eras of joy in chaos are found.
Each quirky find whispers a tale,
Of wild escapades and playful fail.

The Color of Loneliness

Once I painted my walls in blue,
Thought it'd brighten a gloom or two.
But each stroke made my heart feel stuck,
Now my cat won't stop giving me luck.

Chairs from the thrift shop play hard to get,
Each one is a story I can't forget.
I draped them in laughter, what a sight,
Guess they're shyer at boisterous nights!

A vase filled with wilted blooms,
Held together by laughter, love, and gloom.
It leans a bit, but that's just fine,
It's the thought that counts in this heart of mine.

Jackets on hooks, all my friends seem late,
Did they see the sad paint, or change their fate?
Just me and a sandwich sharing a chair,
In the color of loneliness, we make a pair.

Boundaries of the Heart

She said, 'Don't cross that imaginary line!',
But tripped over it while sipping wine.
Now we're tangled in laughter, what a mess,
Boundaries blurred, what more could you guess?

He painted my world in daring hues,
Yet spilled his paint and ruined my shoes.
Now at art class, we giggle and twirl,
With splatters of colors and a dance like a whirl.

The line was fine, then a wild chase,
Slipping and sliding, we found our place.
Pillow forts built with laughter and sheep,
In the boundaries of the heart, secrets we keep.

With sketches of dreams in pastels and more,
We tread on love, always willing to explore.
So here's to lines we may never redraw,
In the chaos of life, we find the awe.

Muffled Conversations

Behind closed doors, the whispers play,
Echoes of laughter, never decay.
A joke so old, it's lost its charm,
Yet we're still giggling, what's the harm?

The cat rolls by with a fluffy sigh,
Joining the gossip, oh my, oh my!
Silhouettes dancing in the soft light,
Who knew secrets could be such a delight?

Teacups stacked with tales untold,
A mishmash of stories that never get old.
Each clang of the spoon adds fuel to the fire,
Muffled conversations we never tire.

Like static on radio, fuzzy yet clear,
In the hum of our lives, we hold what's dear.
So let them murmur, let laughter be loud,
For in these hushed moments, we stand proud.

The Breath of Old Stories

Dusty tomes in the air,
Whispers of laughter everywhere.
A cat in a hat, what a sight!
Echoes of children late at night.

Grandpa's tales of yesteryear,
Endless sighs mixed with cheer.
He swears he once caught a fish,
But the fish had a villainous wish!

Sticky notes left on the floor,
Crazy doodles, a mind to explore.
A sock on the shelf, what's it for?
Each clumsy step opens a door.

Balloons from parties long past,
A pinata that just won't last.
With every bobble, laughter ignites—
These breathy tales are pure delights!

Lanterns of the Mind

A room filled with giggles bright,
Glimmers of joy shine like light.
Cupcakes dance on the table's edge,
Memories swirl like a happy hedge.

In one corner, a wobbly chair,
A pair of shoes with tales to share.
Lamp shades wearing silly hats,
Chasing shadows like playful cats.

Silly socks, mismatched and proud,
Jokes whispered beneath the crowd.
When did we wear those clowny shoes?
The mementos joke, they just won't lose!

Old photographs frazzled and torn,
Captured smiles, hearts reborn.
Laughter echoes, a lanterns' glow,
Shining bright on the paths we know!

Sanctuaries of Remembrance

A closet full of noise and glee,
Where every sock sings music free.
Toasters toast with a little dance,
Every bite a chance for romance.

In corners, old toys with some flair,
Teddy bears and silly hair.
A record spins tales of the past,
Chuckles and memories—oh what a blast!

Nostalgia drapes over the floor,
With sushi pillows and a sock drawer war.
Every corner holds a secret shared,
From racing cars to the stories dared.

Rewinds play when daylight fades,
Each whimsy tale never degrades.
In this sanctuary, joy sparks anew,
For every moment bursts through!

The Tapestry of Lost Moments

A quilt stitched with ghostly sighs,
Each thread holds laughter, never lies.
Pancakes flipped in a kitchen race,
Syrup drips, adding to the grace.

Old board games stacked in a pile,
The cat claims victory with a smile.
Doodle bugs across the wall,
In this patchwork, nothing is small.

Funny faces in frames that grin,
Each captured moment pulls you in.
A pie that spilled, oops on the floor,
Every mess just opens a door!

The stitches hold tales of delight,
Woven memories that feel just right.
In the tapestry, we find our place,
A funny dance in time and space!

Echoes of the Past

Old socks in the drawer, they dance with glee,
Whispering secrets of laundry history.
The toaster pops toast like it's got a dream,
While crumbs pile up, forming quite the team.

Grandma's old chair, squeaks like a song,
It tells funny tales, a little bit wrong.
The cat in the sun, sprawled out on the floor,
Thinks it's the king, but it's just a bore.

The fridge hums a tune, a disco delight,
While yogurt containers have their own fight.
The clock on the wall ticks only for laughs,
Mocking my plans as time quickly halfs.

Memories float like balloons in the breeze,
Holding onto quirks, like cheese with a sneeze.
In this silly space, where laughter ignites,
Even the shadows dance with delights.

Shadows in the Corner

The shadow in the corner wears fancy shoes,
Tapping its toes to its own funny blues.
A pile of old toys hold a wild debate,
Arguing over who was the best at fate.

Dust bunnies gossip, stacked up in rows,
Trading old stories no one really knows.
Under the bed, a sock puppet crew,
Performing Shakespeare with highly fake glue.

The lamp flickers dim, has a giggly fit,
Not quite sure if it's a lamp, or a skit.
The candle wax drips like rivers of goo,
Creating landscapes, where laughs still accrue.

In corners where sunlight timidly peeks,
Playful reflections do funny little tweaks.
Here in the chaos, where nonsense unfolds,
Life's little quirks are the treasures it holds.

Whispers of Forgotten Moments

A slice of cake whispers, 'I'm still a delight,'
Sitting on the plate, embracing the night.
The old TV crackles, tells jokes from the past,
While popcorn kernels escape, oh, what a blast!

Faded photographs giggle in frames,
Capturing laughter, and silly names.
The clock on the mantle, forgets to chime,
Ignoring the years, just stuck at prime time.

The couch springs a tune, oh what a kick,
Chasing away worries, it plays a quick trick.
An umbrella stands proud, like a jester's cap,
Recalling the rain each time it goes clap.

In these fleeting moments, where joy tends to hide,
A dance of delight finds its way to reside.
Echoes of laughter linger like air,
Funny little snippets, floating everywhere.

Portraits in Dust

Portraits in dust, they laugh and they glare,
A family of figures with strange wild hair.
Uncle Bob's mustache, a sight to behold,
Claiming he danced with a bear ever bold.

The old piano sits, dusted with pride,
Whenever it's touched, it begins to slide.
Keys play their secrets, a chaotic tune,
Scaring the cats, making them swoon.

The bookshelf, a hoot, with titles so bright,
Revealing old tales that gave us a fright.
Books leap from the shelves, wanting a read,
Spilling their stories like they're in a creed.

In each little corner, humor unfurls,
Where laughter and dust dance in pirouettes.
Chasing out shadows, with giggles anew,
In this charming chaos, joy sticks like glue.

Stairs to Forgotten Places

Up the stairs where echoes play,
My socks embark on a ballet,
Falling into unexpected spins,
As they spin tales of where they've been.

Each step creaks with a cheeky grin,
Reminding me where mischief's been,
A toy car races down the lane,
With memories of joyful pain.

In the attic, a bicycle waits,
Covered in dust, it contemplates fates,
Last ride was a flop, but oh the thrill,
I flew down hills against my will.

Each landing holds a silly cheer,
Whispered secrets, muffled near,
These stairs hold chuckles, wide and free,
A staircase of sweet, silly glee.

Voices of the Unseen

Chairs giggle at my silly fears,
As I recount my childhood years,
The fridge hums an old, sweet tune,
While socks conspire with the moon.

In shadows where the dust mites roam,
A ghostly laugh feels just like home,
Forgotten toys come out to play,
In this game of hide-and-seek ballet.

A cupboard whispers 'you can't hide',
Behind the pots, strange things reside,
From spoons to forks, they plot and scheme,
In this kitchen, they live the dream.

Voices hum, untold and bright,
Silliness lives in every night,
In corners where the daylight's shy,
Memories wink as they pass by.

www.ingramcontent.com/pod-product-compliance
Lightning Source LLC
Chambersburg PA
CBHW060121230426
43661CB00003B/281